DEVELOPING AND MANAGING YOUR CAREER

WHAT IT TAKES TO GET THAT PROMOTION

by Graham Robert Kingma

Have you ever looked over at a supervisor, manager or executive in your organization and wondered to yourself, *What did she do to get to that position?* We all have. The fact is no one is born with promotion-securing special powers. No one wins some promotion lottery. No one buys a promotion. So what *did* they do?

Managing Your Career is a guide to help you navigate the arduous journey of career development. While there is no simple recipe for a successful career, in this guide you will find advice to significantly improve your chances of professional success. The following situations can be applied to anyone ready to manage their career and start the process of moving to the next level.

Are you ready to start the journey toward that promotion? Chances are, if you're reading this book, you are.

Table of Contents

DEVELOPING AND MANAGING YOUR CAREER

1. Managing Your Career
(Your Other Full-Time Job)
2. Master Your Current Job Responsibilities
3. Acting like a Leader
Will Help You Become One
4. You Are Known by the Company You Keep
5. Do More Than Your Role Requires
6. Know Your Strengths and Weaknesses
7. Make It Known You Want to Go to the Next Level
8. Acting the Part
9. Dealing with a Boss That Is Not Supportive
10. Look for an Opening and Grab It
11. A Little Adversity Never Hurt Anyone
12. When Opportunity Knocks
13. The You in Managing Your Career

1. Managing Your Career (Your Other Full-Time Job)

The most effective way to do it, is to do it
—Amelia Earhart

Developing and managing a career is a full-time job. While your day-to-day focus should be on the requirements of your current job responsibilities, your career must be given the time and attention it deserves in order to reach your long-term goals.

Managing a successful career takes commitment and focus. There are many different elements to moving up the ladder, and those elements are as unique as the people who use them to their advantage. Most people will tell you it's difficult to move up in their industry. When was the last time you heard someone say it was easy to get a promotion at their company? It really doesn't matter which industry you look at as each has its own unique challenges when it comes to getting promoted.

It is important to remember that striving for a promotion is not a goal or interest for everyone. Many individuals are excellent at what they do and are not interested in getting to the next level. Putting forth their best possible effort at their present level is a success in itself. We spend a great deal of our lives at work. If you are happy where you are, don't feel pressured to reach the next level. You should take pride in performing a valuable service to your organization as well as your accomplishments. Being satisfied with your job is a goal we would all like to reach.

Each of us should carefully weigh the pros and cons of a promotion. Ask yourself: How will it affect my personal time? Will I be expected to take special courses at night? Will my working days or hours change as a result of the promotion? On the next page you will find an exercise to help you list the pros and cons of a promotion in your organization. I have listed a few items that you may need to consider. Your first exercise is to add to the list and make it your own!

Making a list like this helps you understand what you are *getting*, and what you might be *giving up* at the next level. If you are reading this book on an e-reader then grab a separate pad of paper for your own personal "Managing Your Career" notes.

Grab a pencil or pen, and let's get started.

If I Get That Promotion

I will get…	I may have to give up…
Good experience in managing people	Just being able to hang out with my work friends as I'll be their boss
More money	My current shift hours and adjust to new shift hours
More flexibility in my job	Some of my personal time when my company needs me on days off

Do you feel you made a complete list? One of the ways to add to the list is by talking to those that have already gone through the experience. Like most things in life, it's always hard to know exactly what the changes are going to be if you haven't gone through the experience. Talk to those around you who have already experienced these changes. Ask them about some of the benefits and drawbacks they experienced after being promoted. The more complete your list, the better you'll understand the changes and the better prepared you'll be for the next steps. Keep the list handy, refer to it often and keep adding to it regularly.

If you've decided you're ready to begin the process of reaching the next level, there are questions you need to consider. There are always a number of people competing for a new job posting and only one person can fill that opening. How do you differentiate yourself from others? How do you ensure you're leading the race when the decision has to be made?

Throughout the book you will be presented with exercises that will enhance the likelihood of you being considered for that promotion. The harder you work on your exercises, the more potential you have to reach your goals. It is important to note that not everyone will be promoted. A good work ethic, special skills, and a higher education among many other elements, may be required to perform the job at higher levels.

Being offered a promotion is one of the greatest experiences you will have in your working career. The more effort you put into reaching your goals, the more likely your goals will become reality. Let's get you ready to reach the next stage in your career.

2. Master Your Current Job Responsibilities

A job worth doing, be it great or small, is worth doing well or not at all.
    −Reed Budge

Your department should have metrics for how they measure your performance. This may be a hassle for many, but you can use these measurement goals to your advantage.

Do you know which metrics are important to your manager and your department? At a minimum your manager and your organization expect you to show up for work on time and complete the job you are assigned to do. What else is expected of you? Which targets can you exceed? If you are allowed to be absent two days a month then would it be better if you only missed one day? Or no days? Do you have a performance target like the number of sales each day? Would it be better to meet these sales goals or exceed them?

Let's do an exercise to make sure we understand what's expected of you in your current job, how you're doing today, and what you could do to exceed those expectations in the future. I have added a few starter items to help you along.

In My Current Job

I am expected to…	Currently I am…	In the future I could…
Be on time for work	Missing about three days a month	Try to be at work every single day unless there is a real emergency
Be on time for my shift	Late about twice a month because of traffic	Leave home earlier for my shift to account for traffic problems
Have a quality score of 85%	Meeting my Quality Score of 85%	Set and achieve my personal goal of 95% every month

Have you captured all of the metrics you are expected to achieve in your job? If you are not sure that you have captured them all, it's time to bring the list to your manager. You could bring only the first column (*I am expected to…*) and make sure you have a more complete list.

How does column one and column two compare? It's now time to make column three your new commitment at work each and every day. Keep

13

the list in a place you can refer to it often. At the end of each week take a look at the list. Ask yourself one question. *Did I reach my new personal goals at work?*

If you consistently achieve your new personal goals then you are on your way to becoming part of a group considered for a promotion.

Are you having trouble consistently achieving your new personal goals? Ask for advice from those around you who are meeting and exceeding what is expected of them. Follow their lead and this may help you in mastering your current job responsibilities. It is worthwhile to take time to explore the reasons for the barriers and make a plan to overcome these obstacles.

Those who exceed their current job expectations have a better chance for opportunities in the future. It should be clearly understood that performing at a very high level in your current position doesn't guarantee you a future promotion. Performing at this level shows the decision-makers you're able to look after your responsibilities well. By rising above the rest in performance, you have started on the path of differentiating yourself from others. Whether you know it or not, when you exceed your job expectations *people notice*.

Decision-makers are influenced by the positive and negative impressions they have of you. The people that will ultimately decide who gets promoted are constantly watching the people in their department.

Unfortunately, it is easier to remember a negative situation than a positive one, and this can hurt you when it comes time to apply. Nyma, an employee with a great deal of potential, could not understand why she didn't get a promotion after doing almost everything right. She had a positive attitude, worked hard, and performed at a high level. Her downfall was the great number of times she was late for work. She had been issued a written warning and felt this was unfair because she performed so well in other areas. Why should something like being late stand in the way of getting a promotion?

All of her hard work was negatively impacted by her tardiness. Nyma needed to erase this perception that people had of her. The perception needed to be erased in order for everyone to see the positive things she could offer at the next position level. She realized that in order to erase this negative impression, she would need to stop being late for good.

Avoid negatives at all costs. Often what you *didn't* do well can be more of an influence on future opportunities than what you *did* do well. Leaders want to promote people who will cause little disruption after promoting them. Nyma realized her good work had been noticed and appreciated. What she didn't realize was that the decision-makers were worried she would set a bad example if she were promoted. It would send a message to others they can be late and still have a chance to be promoted. They weren't willing to take the risk and denied her the promotion.

Nyma made the decision to be on time and even a little early. It took quite a few months to erase the "late" label she had placed on herself. When it was gone, Nyma was seriously considered for the next promotion and was promoted shortly afterward. Nyma turned her negative into a positive and removed the roadblocks to success that were in front of her.

Remember, you are competing with others, and if they have less negative marks against them, you may lose out on the promotion. When you're aiming for that promotion in the future, you need to act as though every day is interview day. Don't say or do anything that you wouldn't do if the decision-maker were standing right next to you. This will help you avoid negative impressions that are so influential when it comes to decisions involving a promotion. By focusing on the positives and avoiding the negatives, you set yourself apart from the rest.

Perhaps you have been an average or below average performer until now. It's never too late to start your career path. In fact, improving your performance can often get you more attention than someone who has always performed at a high level. You will need to perform at a high level for a sustained period of time before you can wipe away any lingering doubts from those that make promotion decisions. In some cases, it can take years to erase the label of an "underperformer." Start *today* and you will eventually erase any doubts about your performance.

Meeting your new personal goals at work is an important element of the journey to your promotion. Be proud of your accomplishments!

3. Acting like a Leader Will Help You Become One

Leadership is the ability of a single individual, through his or her actions, to motivate others to higher levels of achievement.

—Buck Rodgers

If you look to those who have been promoted within your department and the rest of the organization, you will start to see some similarities. In this case, we define a leader as anyone in a role of team leader/supervisor or above.

In a great organization, good leaders act responsibly, look presentable, are honest, cordial, and respect others. They are positive about the direction of the company and have a sense of care and ownership about their contributions. They rarely complain and usually go out of their way to help in any situation. They also go out of their way to speak to everyone in the organization on a more personal level. Great leaders (present and future) know that being kind and respectful to everyone in the organization *no matter what level they are at* is important to the future of your career. Great leaders understand that they need to be as respectful and cordial to the receptionist as they are to the CEO.

This can also mean at times "towing the company line," even if you don't understand or agree with all of the plans for the future. Some individuals complain about changes in policy, procedure, or direction. Future leaders will ask questions to help them understand why the company is going in a particular direction and assist wherever they can. There is a difference between "towing the company line" and agreeing with everything just to get a promotion. Good leaders like to see people who can share their opinions *constructively* while incorporating the goals of the department and the organization.

If you still fundamentally disagree with the plans of your department or company, you have some hard choices to make about whether to stay or leave. Having a positive attitude at all times toward your coworkers and the organization is critical to developing your career path. Great leaders will ask questions instead of complaining. A question of clarification can be a very powerful tool in helping you learn more about why the organization does certain things while showing that you care enough to understand.

Let's try an exercise to help develop your ability to ask the right questions and avoid jumping to conclusions about what you hear at work and helping you keep things in perspective. Let's grab that pencil or pen and get started on the next exercise.

The Issue or Change At My Work Is...

The issue	I could easily complain and say…	I could ask this great question…
From now on, everyone needs to bring a doctor's note when they're sick for two or more days.	*They don't trust us when we say we are sick.*	*I am happy to make sure I bring in a doctor's note from now on. Sick days must cost the company a lot of money. Can you help me understand that part of the business a little more?*
Unfortunately, the holiday party is cancelled this year.	*They just keep taking things away that we enjoy.*	*I understand that cancelling the party must have been a difficult decision. Would you be okay if we organized a little holiday get-together ourselves? We would definitely want you to be there as well!*

Asking the right questions can be a powerful way of learning more about the business and letting the management team know you're interested in their perspective. We are always better off knowing both sides of the argument rather than jumping to conclusions. Learning that the holiday party was cancelled to avoid the manager from having to lay people off might help you understand that it was actually a good decision.

Furthermore, asking questions shows that you have the ability to assess a situation and gather the information needed to make good decisions. This is what great leaders have to do every day when faced with challenges. By asking thoughtful questions you are practicing your skills as a great leader. Along the way your manager will appreciate you trying to understand more. By asking thoughtful questions you will learn more about your organization and the reasons behind the decisions that are made.

When you hear about an issue or change at work, take a day or two to write down some thoughtful questions using the exercise in this chapter. You will be able to use this approach throughout your career. Some of the best executives regularly use this technique to help them clearly and thoroughly understand the circumstances of any situation and provide good judgment to those who rely on them every day.

4. You Are Known by the Company You Keep

It is better to be alone than in bad company

–George Washington

In this chapter we'll take a look at the people with whom you regularly associate at work. Are they considered by their superiors to have a positive or negative attitude toward the organization? Have any of them been recently promoted?

Alyssa wanted to get ahead in her department. The group she associated with was generally filled with complainers and those who didn't always follow the rules or meet the requirements of the job. Alyssa wasn't necessarily negative herself and her performance was actually quite good. Unfortunately, she was labeled as someone who agreed with the group's attitude toward the company because of her association with them. Unfair yes, but the reality is that perception can be a strong force in the decision-making process.

Alyssa had to break free from this group in order to start her career advancement. This was difficult to do and the group gave her a hard time about it. With some hard work, she earned a promotion within a year and found it more enjoyable to spend time with those with a more positive outlook and attitude. After changing the people she associated with, Alyssa noticed her own drive and motivation greatly improved. The effect the negative group had on her was greater than she'd realized. Negative people are very good at pointing out the negative in everything. Pointing out the negatives in a situation is actually very easy to do. Looking for the good in things improves your own attitude as well as the attitude and morale of those around you. Alyssa realized this group loyalty to her was conditional upon listening to and tolerating their complaints. She realized they weren't very good friends after all, when they didn't support her decision to try to advance her career. They tried their best to make her doubt herself.

Leaders within organizations will generally not hire those who don't bring a positive and constructive attitude to the job. Why would they want someone like that around? Leaders want to create an environment that's positive, and they know an important part of reaching this goal is to hire those with a good attitude overall.

If you are not a positive supporter of your organization, you most likely won't see a promotion in the future. Are you helping those around you become better? Are those around you helping to improve your well-being? People often overlook the benefits of associating themselves with the right crowd. Who is the decision-maker in your department? Who are their favorites? These are the people with whom you are better off associating. The obvious advantage is that you will be seen to be associating with those making a positive contribution to your department. In addition there are two other advantages: one, you will be able to learn from those who are looked upon as good current and future leaders, and two, these are the people who the decision-makers will go to for suggestions regarding who to promote next. If you've done things right, your name may float to the top of the prospect list because you've invested in this area.

Associating yourself with the right people doesn't stop at the doors to your department. To whom do you go to for advice about your job and your career outside of your department? Who would you consider to be your career mentor(s)? in other parts of the organization or outside of your organization? You likely already have people you rely on for advice. It is critical to have great mentors you can rely on for career advice and advice on how to deal with challenging situations at work. Anyone can give advice, and they are usually happy to share their thoughts. But is it good advice? Have the people you call mentors succeeded in their careers? Are they dealing with challenging situations well?

Having an A-list of mentors will help you in almost any situation at work. What is an A-list mentor? An A-list mentor is someone who has had or is having a successful career, someone who makes good decisions in difficult situations. An A-list mentor is someone who is comfortable sharing constructive feedback with you and provides you with challenges to help improve both you and your career path. An A-list mentor takes their role as your mentor very seriously and is always looking out for your best interests. Let's grab that pencil or pen and get started on another important exercise.

My Mentor List

My current mentor is...	I go to them to...	Are they an A-list mentor?
My old high school friend because she was really popular	Get some advice on how to deal with my boss	No, she is not happy in her job and has worked for three companies in the past two years.
An uncle because he owns a medium size business	To learn more about important business decisions	Yes, he takes the time to show me the reasons why he makes a certain decision and takes the time to challenge my thinking about my career. He is always encouraging me to work hard and stay focused.

How does your list of mentors compare to an A-list? Could you improve your list of mentors to better help you along the way in your career? If the answer is yes (and it almost always should be!), then let's explore some ways to find an A-list mentor.

Every successful person has A-list mentors, people they can go to for different kinds of advice. Many of those same successful people are very happy to be mentors to others. Your potential A-list mentors are not going to come to you and offer their services. They need to be asked for the favor.

Take a look at your list in the exercise above. Think about who could be your A-list mentor. Is there someone in another department in your organization whom you admire? How about your CEO? Is there a relative or a friend who has done very well in their career? Are there organizations in your community that you could join such as a women in leadership group or a public speaking group that could attract a great list of mentors? Finding a group of A-list mentors is hard work, but well worth the effort when you look at the impact they will have on your career.

Okay, so you've probably thought of one or two (or more) mentors you would really like to have. How do you approach them? What would you say? How would you describe what you are asking of them? What if they say no?

Take some time to write down who you would like as your A-list mentor and why you thought of them. When you have completed your list it's time to write down what you would say once you have a chance to sit down with them. One suggestion is to write it in the form of a letter.

Dear Ms. Lopez,

I want to thank you for taking the time to meet with me. I know your schedule is very busy. I have really admired what you do and your leadership style. I am looking for someone whom I greatly respect who can meet with me a few times a year to help me with my career aspirations. I can't think of anyone I would rather have as a mentor than you. Would I be able to take advantage of some of your valuable time to help me learn from your experiences?

Sincerely;

_____

It is likely some of the people you ask may say no because of personal reasons. It's important not to take this personally. Some will say yes which means that you will be on your way to learning from experiences and advice that will greatly help you in your career. This learning is invaluable!

When your A-list mentor says yes, make sure you remember they're donating *their* time to *you*. Send them a *handwritten* thank you after they say yes. Let them know how excited you are. Gifts aren't necessary; a note tells your mentor that you really appreciate their time and effort. A thank you card once a year around the holiday season is also a nice touch.

Organize four to six meetings with your mentor throughout the year. Pre-booking the meetings shows you're serious and also allows your mentor to organize their schedule. There will always be changes to these dates and times, and you should take these scheduling changes in stride. Always come to these meetings prepared with well thought out questions and situations on which you would like advice. Ask your mentor for projects or exercises you can complete for the next scheduled meeting. Make sure you complete these exercises and projects. This is critical. If you mentor sees you're not taking the sessions seriously he or she will lose interest, and you will lose your A-list mentor.

Continue to add to your list of mentors. You will find you will go to different mentors for different kinds of advice. Having diversity of opinion is always beneficial in your career. You can then take the advice, integrate it into your own experiences and hone your ability to make sound career decisions.

Lastly, with respect to your mentors, it's important to keep in mind that they are not there to find you a job or get you a promotion. It's perfectly fine to show your mentor a specific job posting and ask for some advice on the right approach to applying for the role. Don't expect your mentor to go out of their way to get you the promotion. You should never ask them for these types of favors. If they offer to help then feel free to take full advantage! Your mentors are there for advice and guidance and to provide exercises and projects that will help you grow professionally. Being mentored is a gift; always treat that relationship with respect and professional courtesy. If you treat the relationship with respect and care, you will more than likely have a mentor for years to come.

5. Do More Than Your Role Requires

Any supervisor worth his salt would rather deal with people who attempt too much than with those who try too little.
—Lee Iacocca

As we discussed in the first chapter, just doing your job well will not necessarily get you promoted, although it is a great first step!

It is important you get yourself noticed by doing some extras that are over and above your current responsibilities. Have you seen something that might save the organization money? Are you offering your skills to make those around you better by providing training or assistance? Do you have the opportunity to look after someone's responsibilities while they are on vacation? Perhaps you have some suggestions for improvements to the department. These are important to those running your department, and you will, in most cases, be noticed and rewarded.

Karen decided she was ready for the next level and thought about ways to get noticed. She had some thoughts about how to improve things in her department. Karen decided to pull one of the department heads aside to share her ideas. She suggested a change to a current policy she felt was unfair and had no benefit to the people in the department. Unfortunately, the suggestion wasn't received very well and she was brushed off. Karen was devastated, and it took her a while to understand what had happened. She advised her mentor about what had happened, and he helped her gain the insight that she had come across like a complainer because she had not taken the time to understand the reasons behind the policy. She had not asked the right questions.

As it turns out, there were good reasons why the policy had been implemented. Karen had asked the right questions this time. She gave this a lot of thought and consideration for several weeks and was able to provide some helpful suggestions on the topic, while still respecting that the policy needed to stay. Karen apologized to the department head for her previous approach and asked for a few more minutes of her department head's time. Karen reviewed her suggestions and explained how she had considered all aspects of the original policy decision. Part of her idea was implemented, and she received the credit for moving the department in a positive direction. She had shown support and found a way to contribute her own energy and effort towards a better solution.

The mistake Karen made the first time was that she had assumed she knew everything about her department. By taking the time to learn more about particular areas of her business, she was in a much better position to share her ideas. The information she gathered for her research on the policy did not cost her a cent. Karen benefited a great deal from educating herself about her department and ultimately she showed the decision-makers she had some great ideas. She was also able to show her interest in helping the company improve overall. Even if her ideas had not been adopted, the fact is Karen showed great initiative, which would help contribute to reaching her career goals.

If you're not sure about whether your ideas are good, run them by your mentors. They may be able to add some insight to your suggestions. Some would call this "managing up" or the ability to influence change with those you report to in your department. Good managers appreciate people going the extra mile to improve things in their organization. These are the people who help make managers (and above) look good. When considering promotions, managers usually look first to those who will make them look good in terms of future performance. That's just human nature. This is extremely important to remember.

Ask the decision-makers how a particular project is going—something you know is important to the department. Ask them if there is anything you can do to help out. Offer to use your own personal time whenever necessary. This commitment will be remembered, even if you're not asked to do something specific. Let's grab that pencil or pen and get started on another career development exercise.

How I Could Contribute More?

An important initiative in my department is…	How I am contributing today...	How I could contribute to improvements…
We have been asked to be more efficient when dealing with a certain kind of call.	I am trying to rush the caller to meet my goals.	An improved approach might be to do the administration part of the call on the overnight shift when they have extra time. That way the actual call will take less than half the time.
We have been asked to improve our sales performance.	I am meeting my sales goals.	I could put together my top five ways to improve my selling techniques and offer to give this to my manager to share with everyone.

When you have written down a few items, make sure you take the time to run it by your mentor. It will be a great topic for the two of you to discuss, and they will be able to provide some advice on how to approach your boss with your ideas and willingness to do more. When you are ready, let the people in your department know about your great ideas. You will be appreciated for your thoughtfulness and your efforts.

What if your ideas are not implemented, even though they are great ideas? There may be good reasons why your thoughtful ideas are not being considered. Perhaps use this as an opportunity to thank your boss for considering the idea, and ask if they would be willing to meet so you can better understand why the idea may not be able to be implemented at this time. Your mentor can help with this approach and whether the timing is right. Your ideas may not be adopted, but you *will* be remembered as someone who is trying to make improvements.

Doing more sometimes means contributing your time to your company's events. The company events are usually outside of your work hours. Remember that getting that promotion is your other full-time job. Make the time to demonstrate your commitment. There may even be opportunities to contribute your time to help with the event, further establishing yourself as an important contributor to the organization.

A great deal of planning goes into organizing large events. People will notice when you're not there so plan to attend them and make it a priority. Remember to act responsibly and professionally at all times, especially at more "relaxed" company events.

Company events are an excellent time to meet the executives in your organization. The senior leadership team is often more approachable and more open to conversations with you compared to when you see them in the hallway in the middle of a busy day. It's a chance to try out some of the questions you have compiled and perhaps even identify a new A-list mentor to approach.

Through this journey you will find yourself with opportunities to produce something (whether it's a project, volunteering of your time, or writing a "top five" list). When you are asked to do something extra, show your appreciation. This is, after all, a free opportunity to show off your skills. Throughout your career it is important to remember that no matter how big or small the task or project, take it seriously and present an excellent piece of work. The work you produce reflects your personal brand. Ask for feedback along the way to ensure that you're headed in the right direction. If your work requires spreadsheets, ask a spreadsheet expert to review before you submit. If your work requires a presentation then practice over and over again beforehand. Have someone review your document for spelling and grammar to ensure you submit something polished and professional. You will be remembered for the work you have done and the level of professionalism of your presentation. Always keep in mind that the work you produce is a legacy of your personal brand. Make it as excellent as you are.

Doing more than your role requires takes extra effort and time. The payback for this investment is the goal of a promotion. Along the way you will have opportunities to volunteer for additional responsibilities and produce some extra projects. You will gain new experiences and skills that will help you improve your abilities at work. All the effort can result in a great investment in *you*.

All of these overtures show that you are committed to the organization's success. This should give you a competitive edge when the decision to fill a position comes up.

6. Know Your Strengths and Weaknesses

To improve is to change; to be perfect is to change often.
−Winston Churchill

Continually improving yourself is an important lesson in life and an important element in managing your career. We all have a pretty good idea of what our strengths are. Why? Because it's easy for people to share what they admire in someone (she's so smart, he's so handsome, she's such a great writer, he's really good with spreadsheets). But what are your weaknesses? These are areas we are less open to hearing about and others are less likely to share with us. Why? Because these are difficult conversations to have. Most individuals would prefer to avoid these discussions. For those who are focused on a promotion this becomes a necessary requirement of the journey. You need to find the answer to this question: *What professional areas do you need to improve upon in order to improve yourself overall?*

Your mentors can help in this area. It is also important to have an open dialogue with the decision-makers in your department about their perception of what you can improve upon. This approach will go a long way in terms of helping you improve yourself overall as well as contributing to a possible promotion. Your career development journey starts by understanding what skills and characteristics are required of someone at the next level of responsibility (for example, a supervisor role) and how those compare to your *current* skills and characteristics. The time to find out these gaps is *before* you apply for a promotion. This is one of the most difficult things for people to do, since it's not easy to hear constructive criticism.

If you are open and honest with your questions, be prepared to hear some frank answers. You may not like to hear about your shortcomings and weaknesses, but honest feedback will help you get ahead of others who *are* afraid to ask. It is important to remember we all have things we need to work on. It's a fact and this fact applies to every one of us—no matter what level we're at. Ask a CEO if they're still working on improving themselves professionally, you may be surprised to hear that all of them are working on many areas of self-improvement. The journey of self-improvement never ends. Every great leader has, many times during their career, had to make improvements and adjustments in order to become better. There are no natural born leaders. Every great leader has had to work hard for their leadership skills and accomplishments.

By becoming aware of those areas you need to improve upon, you will have a better understanding of what you need to work on to reach the next level. The more clearly you understand these areas of opportunity, the more clearly your path to improvement becomes. Simply by asking the question *"What areas can I improve upon?"* you show you're interested in constant improvement. (This characteristic is critical as you move up the ladder in your career.) Decision-makers want to promote people who are open to feedback and are interested in continuous self-improvement.

Let's get started on an exercise to help your personal development. Ask someone within your department who has influence in the promotion decision to tell you what you need to work on in order to be considered for the next level role. Write them down here:

Things I Need to Work On

I need to work on this area of professional development	I can improve this area by…	Someone who does this well today is…
I need to act less shy in group discussions.	I could take a public speaking course to help me with my confidence in front of people	A colleague in another section of my department
I need to learn how to use a spreadsheet program.	I can find an online course to teach me.	One of the people in the accounting department that I am already friends with

Write down all the constructive criticism you hear and use this as your training manual for the immediate future. Perhaps there are some courses you need to take or some extra projects you can take on. Maybe there are some tips on a more personal level that will help you be considered for future opportunities such as performance, presentation, and attitude. It is critical to remember that these are very difficult conversations to have for both you and the person giving you constructive feedback. By letting the decision-maker know that you are open to any and all feedback, you will make it easier for them to tell you the whole truth.

Use your list to determine what you can do to improve and who you can seek advice from on how to meet your goals. You may be inclined to ask your mentor for training on how to use a spreadsheet program. It may be more appropriate to find other ways to learn and ask your mentor if those choices make sense. The spreadsheet expert in accounting may be a better choice, as they may be more than happy to give you a few hours of free training.

Many times the pieces of constructive feedback you hear will be things you're already aware of. When you knot the things that may be hindering your career development, you're in a better position to do something about them. This is a great position to be in. Listen to the feedback and address the things you believe you need to improve upon.

The list may be longer than you anticipated. This is a good thing. Pick one or two items on your list and focus on those areas first. Just improving in a few areas can make a significant contribution to your professional development. Think of this as a lifelong journey and not something similar to cleaning out the storage room. Focus on a few things and continue to work through your list.

Schedule regular updates with your decision-maker. As an example, they will want to hear you have decided to take a public speaking course based on their feedback. Let your decision-maker know when you have completed each part of your personal development as well. This shows that you take direction well and are willing to do whatever it takes to reach the next level. This is a characteristic that is looked upon very favorably when people are considered for promotion. Those with influence will know you are constantly improving yourself and will keep you in the forefront of their mind for future opportunities.

7. Make It Known You Want to Go to the Next Level

What would life be if we had no courage to attempt anything?
−Vincent Van Gogh

At this point you may have an idea of which role you would like to have as the next step in your career. It is now time to evaluate some of these roles more formally. Let's get started on an exercise to help you evaluate your next role.

The Next Job I Want

Title of job	
Possible shift days/hours	
Salary	
Have I studied the job description? **(From HR or recent posting)**	
Have I talked to my A-list mentors about this role?	
Have I talked to the hiring manager about this role?	
Do I know what I need to work on to be considered for this role?	
Have I spoken to HR about this role?	
Have I spoken to someone currently in this role to better understand the pros and cons of the job?	
Have I spoken to someone currently in this role to understand what he or she did to help them get the role?	
Will I know exactly when this role gets posted?	

The list is not limited to these items but these may help you get started in compiling a list of roles for which you would like to be considered. The longer the list the more likely you are to be properly prepared when the job becomes available. You may have a few job lists like the one above because you are thinking of applying to more than one role in your organization. While this is a good exercise, try to limit the number of roles you are considering. This will help you focus your attention. Applying for every position that becomes available may send the message that you are not sure what you want to do next.

Jonathan had been doing a great job for a number of years in his role. He loved the company, and it showed in his work. He acted professionally at all times and did whatever it took to help the company improve. Much to his chagrin, another coworker was promoted to the role of supervisor, and, understandably, he wanted to know why he wasn't considered or chosen. Jonathan knew his job performance was good and he had a great attitude at work. He asked the department manager why he hadn't been chosen for the promotion. When Jonathan was asked where his application was, he admitted he had never applied. He just thought he would be offered the promotion if he worked hard.

The fact is that Jonathan was never going to be promoted because no one knew he was interested in a promotion. He thought his hard work and great attitude were enough. Unfortunately, it is rare that an organization will identify and groom future leaders. Most of the time it's up to the individual to let the right people know you're in the race. Asking the right people about future opportunities will help place you in a group of people to be considered for future promotion. Like Jonathan, you need to be performing well at your current job responsibilities and acting like a future leader before you take this step.

It is also important to remember that you may have to "put in your time" before you can apply for a promotion. Leaders want to see you can do the current position well for an extended period of time before they will consider you for the next level. The amount of time varies by company and the responsibilities of your current position. You may need to perform well in your current position for a year or two before taking the important step of letting people know you are interested in the next level of responsibility. The satisfaction of your career will be determined in years and decades. The journey may seem slow but it will go by quickly. Take your time, be patient and you will be rewarded in the long run.

Remember to have regular dialogue with the decision-makers in your own department as well as the others on your list. When was the last time you dropped by to say hello to influential people in those departments? It only needs to be about once a month to let them know who you are. This is an opportunity to ask them about current company projects and learn more about your department's challenges. You may be able to use this information when making suggestions for improvements and perhaps be remembered as someone who can make a difference.

By being known by those with influence, you are differentiated from others who may also want that promotion down the road. It's important to remember to be brief, positive, and to thank them for their time. When done right, this is called networking, and can go a long way to helping you get to that next level. Your mentors will have some great advice in this area since they will have experienced this from both perspectives.

8. Acting the Part

When I see a bird that walks like a duck and swims like a duck and quacks like a duck, I call that bird a duck.
—James Whitcomb Riley

How we act has a lot to do with how we are perceived. Notice I used the word *act*. Of course work is not a movie or a stage, however there is a lesson to be learned here. How we act at work influences the perception others have of us. Acting appropriately at work has a great deal to do with the culture of your workplace as well. Is the leadership team reserved or outgoing? Does your work culture encourage certain types of behavior and discourage other types?

This is not about pretending to be someone you're not. This is about assessing how you portray yourself at work and determining whether this is contributing to your career aspirations or not. You may love to dance at the nightclub on weekends, but it may not be wise to start dancing that way in a team meeting or even at the holiday party.

Antoine worked for a well-known retailer and was regarded as someone who did the frontline job well. He was reliable and gave extra support to others whenever he could. He was the model employee during his shift. Antoine could not understand why he was being passed over for supervisor jobs as he felt he was doing all the right things to get the role. He finally got the courage to go to another supervisor who he respected and asked her what he could do to improve his chances. He was surprised at the answer. The feedback was not constructive criticism of his performance during his shift. It turns out the way he dressed before and after his shift was creating a perception that he was not responsible enough for the role. The car he drove (or more precisely what he had done to the car) also negatively contributed to his image at work. He had "suped-up" his car and everyone in the store could hear the exhaust rumble when he arrived and left each day. He had to re-evaluate his priorities to make a decision on which was more important to his future and his goals. He decided he wanted to invest in his career and was ready to make some changes.

Six months later Antoine had invested in a new car—still fun but a lot quieter, and he traded in his wardrobe for something that matched his new style. He thanked that supervisor for being honest with him when no one else was. Antoine did not have to wait until the end of the year to get his first promotion. All that effort was well worth it.

How do we know what image is appropriate? If you look closely, you'll notice that the leaders in most organizations take the time to dress professionally. The way in which you present yourself can go a long way in showing others your potential.

This doesn't necessarily mean buying a new wardrobe of business suits or expensive outfits will secure a promotion. Is there a colleague who manages to dress and act professionally every day? Ask them what their secret is. They'll more than likely appreciate the compliment and share some of their secrets in return. Your image is an element of your personal brand. Taking the time to dress professionally every day contributes to your personal brand every day. Who is the most professional dresser in your organization? What image does that person portray everyday?

Amanda felt like she was going to get a promotion soon. She had met all of her performance goals and made it known she wanted to be the next supervisor in her department. She was sure she had considered everything she needed to in order to be promoted. In her mind there was no one else more suited for the next level. She felt the interview went well even though there were some strange questions about how she got along with others in her department. She knew she got along very well with all the supervisors and managers and confident about her chances.

A week later the announcement came out. Amanda did not get the job. She was shocked and very angry. How could they have made such a poor decision? She stormed into the hiring manager's office and demanded to know why she was not getting promoted. The hiring manager demanded that she leave and come back the next day when she had calmed down.

Amanda came in the next day, sat down, and very calmly apologized for her actions. She explained that she was so excited about the role and had not even considered that it might be given to someone else. She said she respected the position and had already graciously congratulated the person who did get the promotion. Amanda wanted to understand more about why she did not get the role and was embarrassed when she heard the answer. The hiring manager pointed out that on a number of occasions the supervisors had witnesses Amanda yelling at a co-worker in the parking lot. Each instance involved a criticism about something. The hiring manager had even witnessed it herself a few times.

It was explained to Amanda that this is not how leaders in their organization acted. When was the last time she had seen a supervisor, manager or executive yelling or criticizing someone in public? The organization was not about to bring a leader in who acted this way regardless of how good her job performance was. Amanda had some decisions to make regarding her behavior at work, and they weren't going to be easy decisions.

After taking some advice from the hiring manager and talking things over with her mentor, Amanda was determined to change her behavior for good. She met with every single person she had criticized and apologized for her actions. Although it was incredibly difficult to do, she persevered and made amends with all of them. It took a great deal of time for her to prove her sincerity. Over the next six months she even became friends with some of those she had criticized in the past. It turns out she was better at (and really enjoyed) teaching others how to perform best on the job than to criticize them for not performing well.

Twelve months went by with no criticisms in the parking lot (or anywhere for that matter). Her behavior change was noticed and appreciated by the entire leadership team. Amanda had even contributed to the increase in performance of some of her colleagues, a quality so sought-after in a leader. Amanda was approached to apply for a supervisor role that was being posted. She was awarded the new role. Most importantly, her peers applauded the decision and had even asked to be a part of her new team.

How is social media relevant to your perception at work. Does your online image affect your chances of a promotion? The short answer is *absolutely*.

Frank had finally found a company he could be proud to work for. He really liked the products his company produced and loved working with his boss. Frank was well liked by his peers both inside and outside of work. After two years in the same job Frank wanted more responsibility. He had done all the right things, was great at his current role, let people know he was interested in finding out more about a supervisor position and tirelessly worked on improving himself professionally. His coworkers even encouraged him to apply and believed he would be a great supervisor.

Frank went through the interview process and believed he had a real chance at his dream promotion. During his last interview with the HR team he was asked to explain a few things they had noticed about his Facebook profile. Frank had forgotten all about adding most of his department (including his boss and the HR team) as friends on Facebook. The HR team opened up his profile and asked about a photo of Frank standing on top of a police car with a beer in his hand. Frank could not explain the photo; only saying that it was an old photo and he was really embarrassed about it. The HR team thanked him for his time and the interview ended.

Frank did not get his dream promotion. He knew it was because the organization did not want someone who was okay with standing on a police car holding a beer to be in charge of a team at a respectable organization. It would be just as easy for a local newspaper to find the photo and relate it back to the organization. What could he do? The photo was from a few years before, and he was beyond that part of his life.

Frank was determined not to let this stand in his way of his career aspirations. He had invested too much to stop now. Frank spent a few months cleaning up his online profile. Making sure he removed anything that could be considered embarrassing from his profile. He wrote a letter to his boss and the HR team letting them know the photo was very old and very embarrassing, assuring them that his profile was clear and that they would never see any type of similar content that would embarrass him or the organization again.

One of the HR leaders pulled him aside later on that week, thanked him for the letter and appreciated the fact that we've all done embarrassing things, but that we don't necessarily want online reminders of it for the world to see. She also urged him to apply for the next supervisor position when one comes available. Five months later Frank was the newest supervisor in his organization. He also made sure he took his online image seriously from then on. The image of you online is a big part of your personal brand. Have you searched for yourself online to see what appears? Doing this regularly will make sure you always know what others can see about you online.

Let's get started on an exercise to help your personal development. Ask your mentor how you can dress and act more like a leader. You will likely already have some items you know you need to improve upon. Be honest with your list. Only you need to see it! Write them all down here.

Personal Development

I need to get better at...	I can improve this area by...
Dressing more professionally	Ironing my shirts before heading off to work
Dressing more professionally	Buying a few second-hand suit jackets and wearing them on the days I have a team meeting with my manager
Acting more professionally	Cleaning up my work areas and making sure it looks excellent at all times

Dressing and acting successfully does not mean you have to give up your individuality. Dressing and behaving successfully can go a long way to show others how responsible you are. Your hiring managers are looking for candidates they can trust with large responsibilities. Are you demonstrating this level of responsibility every day?

You may be thinking you'll be able to do all of this *if or when* you get promoted. The secret is to do these things now. Acting like a leader will go a long way in helping others visualize you in that future role. Invest in your personal brand and make the decision to promote you, an easy one for your future boss.

9. Dealing with a Boss That Is Not Supportive

Success is not measured by what you accomplish but by the opposition you have encountered, and the courage with which you have maintained the struggle against overwhelming odds.
—Orison Swett Marden

We've all had a boss who makes us wonder how they ever got their leadership role. They are simply not a good leader, for a whole host of reasons. The fact is, they may very well have been very good in an individual contributor's role and consequently elevated to the next level as a result. They could have been promoted at a time when there was very little competition for the role. Regardless of the reason, they're in that role, and it's up to you to adapt in order to be considered for a future promotion.

Characteristics of a bad boss include dishonesty, taking responsibility for the accomplishments of others, a lack of respect for people, insecurity, and flat out abuse (among many others). You will have your own attributes to add based on your own experiences. We have all had a bad boss, and there will always be the chance we will have one in the future. The important thing to remember is that we should not let this get in the way of *our* future success.

Usually you have three choices when you are faced with a bad boss. The first choice is to try and work with your boss, no matter how big a challenge this may be, to find a comfort zone you can both work within. The second choice is to leave the department or organization in pursuit of a more supportive leader. The third choice is to go above your boss and seek support from those in more senior positions (perhaps your boss's boss).

Your mentor can help you navigate this difficult path. They will have their own "bad boss" experiences and may share how they successfully (or unsuccessfully) navigated their way through the situation. When you are bringing your questions to your mentor, be sensitive to the fact that your approach can easily be perceived as complaining. Remember, complaining about your boss will get you nowhere and your mentors could lose respect for you. This is an opportunity to present some facts to your mentors about situations you've experienced with your boss. You have chosen to approach your mentors in confidence to ask them for some advice on how best to deal with these difficult situations. Listen to the advice carefully and try the advised approaches and suggestions. The relationship will likely not get worse; and you may even find that the relationship with your current boss improves.

In addition to your mentors' advice, try to talk with your boss and find out if there are things you can do to assist them in helping accomplish *their* goals. Most people appreciate an offer for help. Try and build a decent relationship with your boss (as hard as this may be to do). The fact is, if you succeed in improving the relationship, your chances of a future promotion may also improve. When you apply for a promotion, the first person to get a call about you will be your current boss. What will they say about you? Even if you don't describe your current boss as "bad," there may still be characteristics of your current boss that make it difficult or challenging to work within their leadership style.

Let's get started on an exercise to help use these characteristics to your advantage in the development of your career. Ask your mentors for some help with the second column if you have challenges coming up with solutions.

Working with My Boss

It's a struggle because my boss…	I can deal with this better by…
Points out what I could do better in front of my co-workers	Asking her for regular updates on my work when I am alone with her
Always seems like she's in a bad mood on Mondays	I could bring her a coffee once in a while on Mondays and just say a quick hello
Insults some of her co-workers in front of us	Ignore the insults and make sure I never repeat these words to anyone

At some point you need to determine whether your boss will assist you or will try and stifle your development. If your boss is unwilling to work with you to develop your skills and cannot give you a good reason why, then you may need to turn to your mentors for additional advice. Choose the people with whom you can confide and remember that your boss may find out about your conversations with others. The reality is that sometimes you have no choice but to communicate with others if your current boss is standing in the way of your career development due to their own personal agenda.

Remember, you can learn as much from bad bosses as you can from good ones. Bad bosses teach you all the things you shouldn't do when you become a leader. Great leaders avoid the leadership qualities of bad bosses and emulate the leadership qualities of the great bosses they've had in their career. If you are mindful of the characteristics you *wouldn't* want to have as a leader, you will be that much more effective when you become one yourself.

It's easy and natural to get frustrated with an ineffective boss, just remember that they will not be your boss forever. You can take the current situation personally and allow it to cause you frustration, or you can use the current situation to your advantage in your career development. The choice is yours.

10. Look for an Opening and Grab It

The first one gets the oyster the second gets the shell.
—Andrew Carnegie

Now that you've prepared yourself, you can look for the next job opportunity to open up. Job openings can come at a moment's notice. The larger your department, the more openings generally appear. When there is a job opening that is on your target list and fits your capabilities, apply for it. By applying, you've announced to everyone that you are looking for a promotion. Most organizations don't want to let their best people leave (and at this point in your career development you're proving to everyone that you *are* a great employee by showing the great performance in your current job).

Good leaders will pay close attention to the fact that you have applied. You are letting your organization know you feel ready for the next responsibility. Without the need to say it, you are also letting the organization know you are no longer completely fulfilled in your current set of responsibilities. You're ready for more. There is no need to verbalize this fact; your organization will be well aware.

Most of us have an understandable fear of applying for a promotion. You are faced with the possibility of rejection and perhaps even a little embarrassment among your peer group. Two important things to remember here: 1. All great leaders have been turned down for a promotion at one point in their career (and likely, many times). 2. You will never receive a promotion if you don't apply.

The worst thing that can happen when applying for a promotion is that you don't get the job. If this is the case, you will be no further behind. Having the courage to apply will help in your personal development, so don't be shy. You won't be ridiculed for applying for a promotion. In fact, your real friends at work will have more respect for you, and the level of respect that decision-makers have for you will most likely increase as well.

Read through the exercises you have completed so far. You'll know when you are ready to apply, and your mentors can help give you excellent advice as you navigate this new and unknown path. If you've prepared yourself well, you may even find that you are approached when a job opening may be opening up but hasn't yet been publicly announced. Although this is not always common, it's a good sign your plan is working well.

Waiting for the next role to open up can be a test of your patience. It can take time. Many factors can influence when a job opening becomes available. Retirements, resignations, promotions, terminations, budget constraints, and company growth are just some of the influences that affect how long you may have to wait. The longer you have to wait, the more time you have to improve all the elements of your career development. Review the chapters in this book and continue to improve yourself and your personal brand. Every day you invest in yourself will improve your chances of being selected for a promotion when a job opening becomes available. Managing your career is a marathon and requires the necessary training to be truly successful.

Showing patience during this time will help your cause, showing frustration will hurt it. The job openings will eventually come. Have you done everything you can to be ready when that chance finally comes?

11. A Little Adversity Never Hurt Anyone

The greatest glory in living lies not in never failing, but in rising every time we fail.

–Nelson Mandela

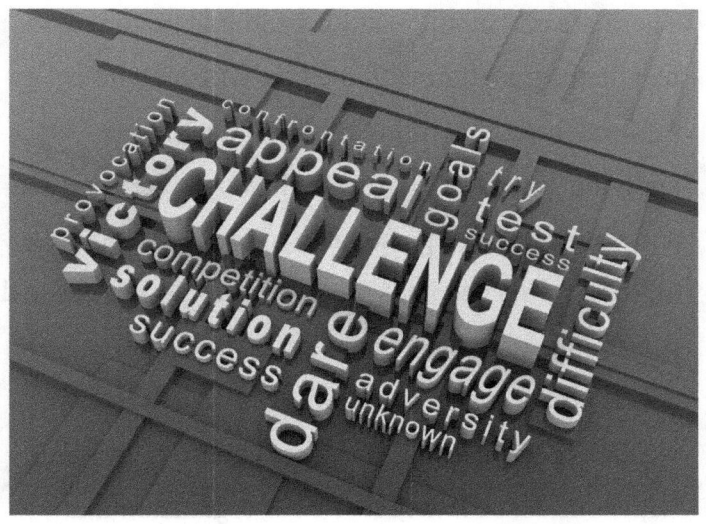

Many of us fail to get the promotion on the first interview. Perhaps it is a little comforting to remember that almost everyone in a position of authority has failed a job interview at one time or another. The reality is that the feelings of rejection are difficult to handle. You may feel the organization is to blame for not recognizing your true talents. In your opinion you were the best candidate, so why couldn't they see it? What is it about you they don't like? These are all natural reactions and it is up to you to handle the rejection with the kind of class and professionalism befitting of the role you were applying for. After all, there will be another opening and you want your personal brand to be excellent at all times. This becomes a great test of your focus and determination. Being turned down for a role can defeat you or make you stronger. This is a moment we *all* experience. Great leaders choose to respond with confidence and focus. Your organization is watching how you react.

How can you use this experience to your advantage? There may be another very strong candidate who gets the promotion before you. So how can you extract a positive from this experience? Well for starters you are no longer competing with that successful candidate the next time a job opening becomes available. Sincerely congratulate the successful candidate and ask them if they would be open to getting together at a later date. Let them know you admire the fact that they were the successful candidate, and that you would be grateful for their advice in terms of learning things that will help you for the next opportunity. The newest member of the leadership team will certainly remember your class and professionalism. They will likely have an influence in future hiring decisions. Turn this experience into an advantage for you and take an opportunity to congratulate someone for a job well done.

It is critically important to seek feedback from those who interviewed you (i.e., what you can do to improve your chances next time). Ask for specifics and be ready to hear some constructive criticism. Write these down and use them as powerful guides in your journey towards professional improvement.

You'll recognize this next exercise from previous chapters. Since you have already improved in those areas (right?) you will need to develop a new list based on the feedback you receive from your interviewer feedback, your mentors, and your own recognized areas of continuous improvement. Let's work on the next set of improvements.

Things I Need to Work On

I need to work on this area of professional development…	I can improve this area by…	Someone who does this well today is…
My answers to the interview questions were not well thought out.	Practicing over and over again	My A-list mentors and others who have developed great interview skills (as well as practicing in front of a mirror)
I need to work on my knowledge of the role I am applying for.	Getting some exposure to what the role requires	Someone who is excellent in the role today

Your mentors will want to know where you feel you excelled in the interview as well as your areas of opportunity for growth. Use this list as your next series of challenges for you to overcome. Don't forget to sincerely thank your official interviewers for the opportunity to apply for the role and present yourself. A brief hand-written letter really goes a long way. After all those involved in the application process gave you a fair opportunity to be in the running for the role.

Accept that it just wasn't *your* time. The reasons they selected another candidate were not personal. How you manage yourself will go a long way to how the hiring manager perceives you. The next interview may hold the key to your success, so be patient. Anything worthwhile in life is going to take hard work, dedication, and perseverance. Showing that you can accept adversity and constructive criticism after the interview will improve your chances even further for the next interview. You have now experienced some of the common interview questions, which means that your answers can only improve during the next official interview.

Madhu noticed a job opening for a supervisor position and decided to apply for it along with two other peers. She felt that some of the training and education she had acquired on her own time would help her get the job over the others. She was terrible in her first interview, and she knew it. She had no idea about the kinds of questions she would be asked and she realized right away that she wasn't prepared for the interview or the job. She then asked for feedback about the interview. She listened attentively and wrote everything down.

The hard part was beginning the process. Not only did she need to come to terms with some of her shortfalls, she also needed to figure out how to improve them. What Madhu didn't realize right away, was that she now had an advantage over others who would be applying for a position in the future. She found her A-list mentors and worked with them to help her sort out where she needed to improve. Madhu drafted her own professional development program based on the interview feedback, advice, and support that she received from her mentors. The work was exhausting, and she realized the other unsuccessful candidate from the previous job opening was not doing any self-improvement at all. This gave her extra motivation to continue.

Six months later another supervisor position became available and Madhu applied with one other candidate. She aced the interview because she was prepared for many of the questions and had practiced her responses. It was very clear to the interviewer that Madhu had worked hard to improve in the required areas; the previous training experience she had gained was a real asset for the role as well.

Without even asking, Madhu's mentor was called for some feedback by the hiring manager immediately after the interview. The mentor explained how dedicated Madhu was to her own professional development. As it turned out, the individual who had also been turned down the last time did not respond professionally after the previous interview and was denied another opportunity to apply. The other individual who applied this time struggled during the interview. He did not have the knowledge Madhu had gained from her previous interview opportunity. Madhu used adversity as a learning opportunity; she made it work to her advantage and became the department's newest supervisor that day.

Turn adversity into opportunity. If you do your due diligence and put forth your best effort, next time it may be you who earns the promotion over someone else.

12. When Opportunity Knocks

In the middle of difficulty lies opportunity.
—Albert Einstein

Sometimes we have to make sacrifices in order to reach our goals. Most often, when a new job opportunity becomes available they are among the least desirable shifts. There may be changes required in your personal life to accommodate the requirements of the next level position. Everyone who has been promoted has had to make sacrifices to get there. To them, the rewards are usually well worth the sacrifices they have to make. Having a balance between work and one's personal life is extremely important, and it helps to have the support of your family and friends.

Tony had worked his ideal Monday to Friday nine to five shift in a frontline position for the past five years and had prepared himself well for the next job opening. His interview went well and he was told there was a real chance he would get the position he wanted. He also realized that the new position was for the evening shift and included a weekend day. Tony had some decisions to make. If he accepted the job, he would have to turn his life upside down to accept the evening shift. After discussing it with his family and getting their support, he was ready to accept the position and all the changes in his life that accompanied it.

Tony got the promotion. He realized there were a few candidates who had applied for the position. He was the only one qualified that was *also* willing to make the hard sacrifices to adjust to the new shift. Tony had made a decision, with his family, to focus on a long-term goal. Tony realized that in order to be promoted he was going to have to make personal changes that suited the company, not him. The changes weren't easy but eventually he adjusted to them. The additional money he now earned helped his family adjust a little bit easier to the changes as well.

Tony now had a new goal: to work towards his ideal shift as a supervisor. He worked hard in the new role and made sure he was considered one of the best in his department through constant personal improvements. One year later, a supervisor position became available in his department with his ideal shift. Tony was next in line and got that position. Someone newly promoted was hired into his old shift. With openness, patience, and some adjustment to his lifestyle, Tony was able to reach his ultimate goal.

Making the decision to accept a promotion should be taken seriously. You'll want to make sure you are set up to succeed in the new role. If your current circumstances do not allow you to take on additional responsibility or a change in your shift then explain this to your hiring manager. They will want the successful candidate's full attention and dedication in the new role.

Sometimes the path to your career goal is not ideal. Talk to those who have already made the sacrifices. How did they manage? What did they learn? You'll realize that they likely had similar challenges and also had to come up with some creative ways to overcome them. Most people in leadership positions get there through sacrifice. Most will tell you it was not easy, and most will also tell you it was well worth it. And most are willing to share these experiences with you if you ask.

13. The You in Managing Your Career

If I have the belief that I can do it, I will surely acquire the capacity to do it, even if I may not have it at the beginning.

–Mahatma Gandhi

Perhaps the most important lesson to remember about managing your career is that no one else will manage it for you. You are in exclusive control of your career. The most focused and determined individuals will likely have the most support in their career journey. You may be lucky enough to have someone in your department who identifies you as a future leader and helps with your promotion. This is rare, unfortunately, and therefore the onus is on you to work hard to achieve your goal.

Managing your career is ultimately your responsibility, and the more you rely on someone else to do it, the better your chances of missing out on your goals. It takes focus, persistence, and energy to climb the ladder. The amount of energy you put into your career is generally the amount you will receive back in terms of success and rewards. Every little thing you do to improve your chances of a promotion is time well spent. As it turns out, these "little" things are not so little after all. Think of every one of your individual improvements as creating distance between yourself and other candidates. Each of these improvements will help you get closer to your goals.

The strategy around getting promoted is a bit like playing a game. You are competing against others to win. There are rules to follow, but the rest is up to you. The more you improve yourself in key areas, the better chance you have of winning that promotion. By adopting the "buck stops here" attitude towards your career, you take ownership of your future. Whenever you start to blame outside influences on why you're not getting promoted, you lose this advantage. By not pointing fingers you keep the control you need to succeed. Remember that you will have improved yourself regardless of whether that promotion comes or not. For this you can feel eternally successful.

Many of the tips you have read will take you outside of your comfort zone. It is easier to do nothing and hope that you are selected for that promotion when a position opens up. Realistically the "hope method" isn't very reliable. Managing your career requires being proactive.

Stepping outside your comfort zone is something you have to face to be successful. Every leader has to do this repeatedly. Every time you do this you will improve your skills and knowledge. Managing your career is your other full-time job, which requires time and dedication to manage it well. Always remember that the people you are competing with for the same positions do not have any secret recipes for success. They have the same challenges you do. By focusing on your own continuous improvement, you not only improve yourself, you also set yourself apart from the rest.

You can liken managing your career to training for a marathon. Every time you improve yourself, you are closer to reaching the finish line. Just because someone else crossed the finish line before you doesn't mean your race is over. Learn from them and keep going. Eventually, with hard work, you will reach your goal as well. After you get that promotion you may find yourself creating a new set of goals as the marathon of your career continues.

The journey to that first promotion is paved with difficulties and challenges. That journey will get more difficult every step you take up the ladder. The opportunities you create for yourself and your path of self-improvement may be worth all of your hard work and dedication in the end. Continuing to improve yourself is an important part of managing your career. You may have improved your skills in some areas, but you can still improve others.

Be proud of your accomplishments and continue to strive for improvement. Always focus on what is most important in life whether you are working towards that promotion or not. We can learn a great deal from those who are nearing the end of their career about life and the importance of balance. As you take the time to more effectively manage your career and your personal development, remember that organizations have a constant need for great people to become great leaders.

Why shouldn't *you* be one of them?

www.ingramcontent.com/pod-product-compliance
Lightning Source LLC
Chambersburg PA
CBHW071303040426
42444CB00009B/1846